Advanced Praise for *Speech Blueprint*

"I love seeing a speech broken down. *Speech Blueprint* is a great book that provides practical insight and wisdom for delivering a clear and effective message. The ten elements that Paul touches on will help shape and reinforce the mindset needed for any communicator. It's a must read!"

— **Paul Martinelli,** President
The John Maxwell Team

"*Speech Blueprint* is a guide for any leader or professional who wants to create and deliver a compelling message. Not only does Paul identify a great speech to learn from, but he identifies the core elements that anyone can use to connect with others."

— **Mark Cole**, CEO
John Maxwell Enterprises

"A great message has a heartbeat. I love the EKG visual that Paul uses to illustrate this point. Speakers speak not just to deliver information, they speak to create transformation, to move us to action. Paul takes us from the starting points of beginning, middle, end to creating a message that touches the heart of the audience. Put these tips to use and you will up level your next speech!"

— **Diane Caine,**
Leadership Coach & Consultant

"Speakers speak, but great speakers have a plan. They don't leave it to chance. To go from good to great as a speaker, you need a blueprint. Paul Gustavson has taken one of the greatest TEDx Talks in history and created a framework for you. Follow Paul's advice and you will be on you way to your next great speech!"

— **Mike Harbour**, Speaker and
Leadership Coach
Author of *Power Principles*

"Paul's thorough approach even incorporates a DISC personality perspective alongside each element of the *Speech Blueprint*. Paul truly wants us to connect with our audiences. His insights work whether your audience is across a conference table or across an entire conference hall."

— **Trudy Menke**
Executive Coach and Trainer
Reframing Leadership, LLC

"*Speech Blueprint* is packed with practical, actionable content from start to finish. What resonated with me most is the chapter titled Frame with Questions. I see this book as a resource to review at least once a year to keep my talks fresh, relevant and valuable for my audience!"

— **Dave Cornell,** Speaker and
Author of *Cultivating Courage*

"Through his work in *Speech Blueprint,* Paul brings to life the hidden gems of a great speech presentation. Using these keys from Simon's TED Talk will expand your opportunities and elevate your connection with your audiences."

— **Joe Dutkiewz**, Founder
Crayon Leadership LLC, and
Spark Consultancy Group

"As a person who has a passion for creating world class content and the art of communication, I was deeply intrigued with Paul's analysis. Taking time to understand what connects an audience to you and your message is the foundation for a great delivery. *Speech Blueprint* will help you craft your message and communicate with clarity and confidence."

— **Roddy Galbraith**
Speaker Trainer
The John Maxwell Team

"Paul is one of the most brilliant, organized, and systematic people I know. Even if you only apply a fraction of what he teaches here, you'll reach levels of success you've never seen before."

— **Dave Gambrill**
Executive Coach, and
Leadership Consultant

"This is a true blueprint of how to craft a speech to connect with your audience and we all want to connect with our audience. Simon's TED talk is a classic and perfect example to use for *Speech Blueprint*."

— **Betsy Hayden**
Motivational Speaker and Executive Coach

"When people think TED Talks, they likely think of Simon Sinek. *Speech Blueprint* by Paul Gustavson is a simple-to-implement analysis of ten elements Simon used - that we also can use. Whether you're a budding speaker or full time, Paul's reverse-engineered playbook will up level your game."

— **Nathan Eckel**
Founder and Host,
BeTheTalk Podcast

Speech Blueprint

Using Simon Sinek's
TED Talk
as a Model to
"Inspire Action"

PAUL
GUSTAVSON

Speech Blueprint –
Using Simon Sinek's TED Talk as a Model to "Inspire Action"
by Paul Gustavson
Published by LEAD EDGE PRESS

LEAD EDGE PRESS
c/o SimVentions
100 Riverside Parkway, Suite 123
Fredericksburg, Virginia 22406

Editorial Review: Joseph and Lisa Dutkiewicz
                    Sue Jones

Cover design: Rupa Limbu

Published in the United States by Lead Edge Press
ISBN: 978-0-9976872-3-1

First Edition – February 2019

http://speechblueprint.com

Dedication

To leadership builders far and wide.

Always Remember:

Your cause is worthy.

Your pursuit is just.

Your words matter.

Always speak life!

Contents

Introduction

S imon Sinek models for us what might be the near perfect speech in his TED Talk classic from September 2009 [1]. His speech is titled "How great leaders inspire action." Have you seen it? To date, there have been nearly 42 million views.

Curious as to why it's been so impactful, I decided to do a deep dive of his speech and break it down into its core components. I wanted to learn what I could to create presentations myself that were at least in the same hemisphere as Simon's.

What you hold in your hand is a result of that work. It is a guide for any leader or speaker who wants to create and deliver a compelling message to an audience. It breaks down for you **the ten essential elements for presenting an idea that inspires action**. Again, it is a based on a tried and true TED Talk, and it's a powerful mechanism that I think anyone can use.

Each short chapter within this book explores one of these ten elements. We also examine how these elements resonate with the four different personality styles representing your audience based on the popular DISC model. This is important, because, as a speaker, your goal is to connect with your audience. Knowing the impact and the value of each element as it relates to the different temperaments of your audience will help you create greater connection.

Within this book, we specifically explore how to create dips and spikes, and why they are important. We discuss the value of questions, and the power of stories. We explore the impact of inserting scientific research and the magic of pauses within our talks. And we also examine how to pivot through a crisis and iterate to drive home a key point. Finally, we talk about using visual tools and creating an ending that always satisfies and leaves the audience inspired.

From Simon's incredible talk, let us now uncover a speech blueprint that nearly anyone can use.

* * *

Note: The appendix at the end of this book provides a full transcript of Simon's TED Talk. I recommend you refer to it as you read this book. In addition, you are highly encouraged to watch Simon's TED Talk, which can be found at http://speechblueprint.com.

Chapter 1

Deliver Dips and Spikes

You can speak well if your tongue can
deliver the message of your heart.

— John Ford

The graph below, reflects the heartbeat of Simon's message. It's filled with dips and spikes, which are paramount for any compelling speech. I call it a Speech Electrocardiogram -- or Speech EKG.

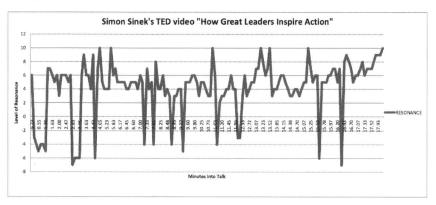

The questions that Simon probes the audience throughout his talk reflect the "dips." They are the downbeats depicted below the midpoint line in the graph. Whereas, the strength of his comments and insights are related to payoffs for the audience, and they can be found above the midpoint line. They are the upbeats. The higher the spike the bigger the payoff.

The dips and spikes of your speech reflect your passion, and the message of your heart. If there are no dips or spikes, then there is no heartbeat to your message. Your message needs a heartbeat – it needs dips and spikes. Otherwise it is dead.

Notice as you look at the Speech EKG, how questions (the downbeats) are used to setup a payoff (the upbeats)? I encourage you to study Simon's speech to learn how to deliver a powerful message to your audience with these kinds of dips and spikes too.

I've put the full context of his speech along with my analysis in the Appendices, so you probably want to take a look at that. This is what created the Speech EKG. Also, be sure to watch his video. Each time I watch it, I seem to pick up something new. I bet you will too.

For example, one thing I saw is that Simon received a 7 or higher on the payoff scale after he probed the audience with a set of questions. It shows how the best upbeats (spikes) always follow the downbeats (dips).

We will explore how to use questions in Chapter 2, and how to use stories, science and humor to create spikes in Chapters 3, 4 and 5. As you study this model and read the rest of this book, the goal for you is not to be like Simon, but to use what Simon has done as a model to shape your message and come across as authentic.

This model is scalable for almost any length of talk and for any audience. It's a powerful way to deliver a message from your heart.

Once again, for details of his speech, be sure to glance at the transcript in the Appendix as you read the rest of the book. It will help drive home the importance of each element as we journey together.

Chapter 2
Frame with Questions

The success of your presentation will be
judged not by the knowledge you send
but by what the listener receives.

— Lilly Walters

O ne lesson from Simon's speech is that we should take time to prompt the audience with questions; questions which are then followed with stories (Chapter 3), or scientific research (Chapter 4). This allows the audience to see the same observations you discovered.

As you look at Simon's transcript, or watch his video, notice how Simon uses questions up front to introduce the stories he later unpacks. Like Simon, I encourage you to use questions to prompt the audience to think. Questions prepare your listeners to receive. Questions create mysteries that audiences want solved and answered.

Let's take a look at the first six questions that Simon asks in the first 90 seconds of his speech:

1. "How do you explain when things don't go as we assumed?"

2. "Or better, how do you explain when others are able to achieve things that seem to defy all the assumptions?"

3. "For example, why is Apple so innovative?"

5

4. "They are just a computer company; they are just like everyone else. Why is it they have something different?"

5. "Why is it that Martin Luther King led the civil rights movement?"

6. "Why is it that the Wright Brothers were able to figure out controlled powered man flight when there were other teams more qualified?"

Then he hooks the audience when he suggests that, *"There's something else at play here!"* This hook proceeding his six-pack of questions prompts the audience to the stories he will later share that answers the embedded question within the title of his speech. *"How do great leaders inspire action?"* What Simon is doing with this set of questions is he is framing the problem that he wants the audience to explore with him before leaping to solutions.

The art of framing is a key component to a great presentation. Author Matthew May calls this *framestorming* in his book *Winning the Brain Game.* [2] According to May, "With framestorming, the focus is on generating questions, not solutions." He adds that, "Framing a problem properly has everything to do with whether it gets solved elegantly." Framing turns a problem that others may be itching to solve, into puzzles that an audience is willing to slow down for and see unfold. It engages the audience.

Framing starts with good questions. Author Warren Berger refers to them as "A More Beautiful Question" in his book with the same name. [3] He shares that, "a beautiful question is an ambitious yet actionable question that can begin to shift the way we perceive or think about something." He adds, that it "might serve as a catalyst to bring about change." Certainly, Simon's TED Talk for millions of viewers has had that type of impact – it's created change for individuals and organizations worldwide.

Framing starts with questions. For instance, Simon uses the phrase "Why is...?" and "How do you...?" in his set of questions. Another great phrase to start with is "What if...?". "What if...?" is the story tellers' question, and stories are what we will explore in the next chapter.

Questions from phrases like these help speakers frame the puzzle they want the audience to see solved. I encourage you to follow this pattern in your own speeches and stories.

It doesn't have to be a six-pack of questions like Simon uses, it can be just one or two. But these types of questions that help frame the problem can be used to set up the stories, share the science, and make your point. In fact, Simon uses the six-pack pattern twice in his speech. The second time it's to frame the value of speech to each person in the audience. He's makes it personal.

1. "By *Why*, I mean what's your purpose?"

2. "What's your cause?"

3. "What's your belief?"

4. "Why does your organization exist?"

5. "Why do you get out bed in the morning?"

6. "And why should anyone care?"

A personalized six-pack like this creates a dip, because it makes people squirm a bit. These are questions directed at our heart. Simon uses them to usher in a big spike that resonates with the audience. Likely the hook he used earlier is what connects our heart to our mind, *"There's something else at play here!"* Can you see the setup he is making for stories, for science, for the key point?

7

One more thing, keep in mind that there are likely a mix of personality styles and learning styles in the audience. On the DISC scale, questions followed by a hook help address the priorities of all personality types.

For instance, those who are high C's value details, which questions help usher in. "C" stands for Conscientiousness. These audience members place emphasis on quality, accuracy, expertise, and competency. Questions help because C's prefer objective reasoning. They often respond well when prompted with a question.

Those who are high I's also do well with questions. "I" stands for Influence. They want openness and they value relationship building. These audience members who are high I's place an emphasis on prompting and persuading others. They often show enthusiasm and like to see it reciprocated. They like to collaborate. This is where questions and framing help.

Good questions also help those who are high D's, because it shows them that you, the speaker, are driving towards a point. "D" stands for Dominance. These audience members place emphasis on accomplishing results, getting to the bottom line, and they value confidence. Questions, ironically, help portray confidence in a speaker. D's also want to see the big picture, and because of that they can be blunt, but just enough good questions help slow down their thinking. It allows them to be patient in a slow reveal of the solution.

The fourth type of personality are those who are high S's. "S" stands for Steadiness. Questions can help the pacing of a speaker and connect with the S's. They like cooperation, sincerity and dependability, and don't like to be rushed. So, when you do ask a question, don't readily respond with the answer. They prefer a calm manner and approach. Allow yourself to wait a little bit. This is where stories can really fit in.

Chapter 3
Follow with Stories

*For me, the best moments in storytelling are the
ones where I feel I'm discovering something.*

— Marcus Sakey

Simon shares four key stories in his speech to help drive home his points: a story about Apple, a story about the Wright Brothers, a quick story about TiVo, and finally a story about Martin Luther King, Jr. Each story shared four essentials: the *hero*, the *dream* they pursued, the *challenge* they faced, and the ultimate *impact* they had on others.

He uses story because our brains are wired to work with stories. It's how we are designed. Often, when a story is told, the audience puts them self in the *position* of the hero who has a *challenge*. Why? Because, as an audience, we have challenges too, and we want to see how the hero rises above the fray in pursuit of their *dream*.

The story of the Wright Brothers also shows the element of *contrast* by comparing someone who had the same dream but missed the mark. Specifically, he shares the story of Samuel Pierpont Langley, who was gifted, had the same dream, was well funded, but lacked the one thing that made the difference. As an audience we want to know what that is.

Earlier he uses this technique of *contrast* with Apple in mentioning Gateway and Dell. Here we have two computer companies, like Apple, who both dove into new markets. Apple found great success with their iPod Music Player. Gateway, who was just as capable, failed to have equivalent success in their pursuit of televisions. Dell met the same unfortunate fate with their music player. Simon uses *contrast* to identify perhaps the most important element of a good story, *differentiation*.

Differentiation is the key to every great story, and every great organization. It's what makes a hero a *hero*. Your story that you share must reveal the *challenge* but also something that shows a different path --a different mindset, a different tact -- than the status quo.

The best stories with differentiation are stories of perseverance where the *hero* faces a problem, yet still holds onto the *dream* and finds a way to pivot and ultimately make an *impact*. Think again of Simon's prime examples: Apple, the Wright Brothers, and Martin Luther King, Jr. Every one of these stories resonates with the audience because they are stories of perseverance describing a *dream* pursued by the *hero* despite the *challenge*.

The truth is, having stories in your back pocket makes it far easier to engage an audience and deliver your point. Speaker great Les Brown shares it this way, "Never tell a story without a point, and never make a point without a story."[4] Take time to explore stories for your speech. Look for a short example tied to your theme and the point you want to make.

Even if your audience may already be familiar with your story; that's okay. Just tell it a little differently. When you share the story, allow them to identify with the *hero*. Let them pretend and see themselves as the hero. Remind them again of the hero's *dream*, share with them the *challenge*, and then show them the differentiation that resulted in the *impact*. And since you are the storyteller, tell it as if you are the guide who had a firsthand view of what really happened. To an audience, the guide always tells the best story.

Finally, remember when you share stories, it allows the audience to see the observations you have discovered. Regardless of the DISC profile your audience might be, we all enjoy a well delivered story. But keep in mind a high D, which stands for Dominance, may not want a long story. They want you to get to the point, but they still like a good story – we all do! And if you frame it right, the D's will be willing to let the story be told.

Chapter 4
Share the Science

There is something fascinating about science.
One gets such wholesale returns of conjecture
out of such a trifling investment of fact.

— Mark Twain

Notice how Simon uses scientific research to back up his observations. He shares about the biology of the brain, and the law of diffusion of innovation. Stories are powerful, but the scientific research provides the proof and evidence that makes it hard to refute.

Unfortunately, scientific research is often the one element a speaker is most willing to punt on and not provide. But punting could prove to be fatal. How can you truly convince someone without some type of scientific proof? Make them believe by sharing hard but simple evidence.

Don't go overboard though. Too much data and details will bore your audience. Fortunately, in Simon's TED Talk, he shares the scientific research at a layman's level – he makes it understandable for almost everyone. He tries not to sound overly educated or assume the audience already has all the knowledge. My recommendation is this; share the research as if you had recently learned it yourself and it's what gave you this awareness that you are passionate about sharing. That's how Simon comes across.

What Simon is doing is sharing insight that maybe half the audience does not know yet. Speakers like Simon recognize that an audience values and appreciates new information. The Heath

Brothers, authors of the bestselling book *The Power of Moments*, call this a Moment of Insight. [5]

For the rest of the audience, the science that Simon shares confirms the insight that they already have, thereby deepening the level of trust. Any time someone echoes a belief or confirms a truth, it arouses interest and causes the other person to pay more attention. Why? Because it satisfies self-interest. The Heath Brothers call this a Moment of Pride. Moments of Pride, which can be accomplished by simply calling someone by their first name, affirms an identity, confirms an insight, or acknowledges an achievement. In short, it satisfies the ego, which subconsciously is looking to be stroked.

As a speaker, your passion tied with the use of science, which creates a moment of pride for the audience, will be reciprocated by the audience. It will elevate their passion and their interest in what you have to say. For Simon, sharing the research insight also solidifies his point. It turns any doubters into believers, and preexisting believers into fans. That's because science persuades.

As you prepare for your presentation, take time to find evidence and proof that you can share too. Keep it soft and easy to understand, but don't be afraid to use it. Remember, it will help you drive your point home more easily. And as you share it, share your excitement along with it, otherwise it will sound boring and you will lose the audience.

Keep in mind again that there are different personality styles and learning styles in the audience. Science and facts help those who are high C's. Again, "C" stands for Conscientiousness. These audience members place emphasis on quality and accuracy, expertise, and competency. Scientific research helps high C's since they prefer objective reasoning. They want the details. Give them just enough.

Chapter 5
Inject Real Humor

*From there to here, and here to there,
funny things are everywhere.*

— Dr. Seuss

S ome of the lighter, yet bigger payoffs, which create connection for the audience, come when Simon injects a little humor into the mix. But he doesn't tell jokes. He uses subtle satire and commentary. Here are a few examples from his TED Talk:

- "The only reason these people buy touch tone phones is because you can't buy rotary phones anymore."

- "We use TiVo as a verb. I TiVo stuff on my piece of junk Time Warner DVR all the time."

- "He gave the "I have a dream" speech, not the "I have a plan" speech."

These satire statements and commentary each create a well-timed laugh for the audience, because they resonate with their feelings and observations. Share something ironic with an element of truth. This is what usually works best in creating humor.

One key to creating humor is not to take yourself so seriously. Have fun poking at odd behaviors of others, including yourself. And be sure it ties somehow to your stories and research.

Keep in mind once again that there are different personality styles and learning styles in the audience. Speakers able to offer some humor and levity resonate with almost everyone, but this is especially true of those who are high I's.

"I" stands for Influence. These audience members place emphasis on influencing or persuading others. They encourage openness and relationships. They often show enthusiasm and like to see it from others. Remember, they are optimistic and like collaboration, this is where humor helps, because a good laugh brings people together. They also dislike being ignored, and humor is the antidote to being ignored.

Finally, I want to share some advice from speaker great and comedian Ken Davis. As you contemplate inserting humor into your speech, take stock in this definition. *"Humor is a way of saying, "I'm not okay and you're not okay, but that's okay,"* [6]

Davis points out how humor is an effective element for a speech, because "it softens the heart". When you point out the funny oddities of life – especially the ones you have experienced. It has a way of softening people, and they become more receptive to your message. Humor also provides a way to get instant feedback.

Lastly, Davis emphasizes that what makes something funny is a mix of "The Truth" and "Ridiculous Exaggeration." Most likely, you've seen enough of the world to share a few examples that satisfy both of these. Find a creative way to use one in your next speech!

Chapter 6
Insert Timely Pauses

The most precious things in speech
are the pauses.

— Sir Ralph Richardson

One of the things that you might not readily notice is the amount of pauses Simon uses in the delivery of his TED Talk. Sometimes his pauses are subtle, meaning they're not very long, yet he uses just a bit of hesitation -- sometimes in the middle of a sentence -- to make sure the point is being driven home.

In his TED Talk, Simon also uses pauses before and after a question, after a satire statement of humor, or when he makes a key point. The pause allows the thought to penetrate into the audience. It allows them to respond with emotion. He doesn't wait too long for the response, just long enough to give you time to think.

You and I can try this same technique. It's not always the words of what we say, it's how we say it using well timed pauses and maybe even a facial grin for emphasis.

Think of it this way. A speech is really a dialog with another person. It's two ways – even though one person seems to be doing all the talking. For there to be a connection between you and your audience, you need to pause, look into their eyes, and allow them to synch with the thoughts, ideas and questions you deliver.

Pulling on this further, when you pause, recognize the opportunity it creates for the audience to ponder what you have said, and subtly communicate back to you. In their mind they are quietly forming words of thought agreeing (or in some cases disagreeing) with your point.

You are inspiring action, and that always starts with thought -- not just yours, but theirs too; they have the final word. Only in the pauses will real connections happen. Don't go overboard, but short little moments to synch can make all the difference. And in the pauses, watch for the non-verbal and facial response. They will give the feedback you are looking for.

Next time you watch Simon's talk, observe how he uses pauses to allow the audience to stay in tune with him. Like an orchestra composer, he controls the tempo of thought for the entire audience. The audience is his orchestra, and he's the conductor. It's beautiful to watch.

For you to see the impact of what Simon is doing, you can measure it by the amount of times you either nod your head in agreement or have the urge to jot down what he says. The pause is the key. In fact, note takers love speakers who pause, because it gives them a chance to jot down the thought.

Keep in mind again that there are different personality styles and learning styles in the audience. Speakers who are able to offer timely pauses resonate the most with those who are high S's. "S" stands for Steadiness. These audience members place emphasis on cooperation, sincerity and dependability. They don't like to be rushed. They prefer a calm manner and approach. They thrive on supportive actions.

Pausing creates pacing for you and your audience. You don't want to leave them behind.

Chapter 7
Pivot Through Problems

If you want to achieve something,
you're going to run into roadblocks, but you have
to learn how to pivot and explore your options.

— Hannah Bronfman

What I love about Simon's TED Talk is that it's far from perfect. If you noticed, there were some technical difficulties that Simon faces in the middle of his talk. As you watch the video you can see that his audio has a major glitch – and it gets progressively worse. Eventually, he is handed a new mic.

Despite the trouble with the audio, Simon doesn't let it affect him. Again, like a conductor, he simply pivots along the way and never loses site of the goal to share his message and connect with the audience. Therein lies the key.

His focus at the start and throughout his talk was to make sure he had a connection with the audience with a simple message. When you have that kind of focus, even if there are technical difficulties you too can find a way to brush off the distractions.

A few years ago, I had a chance to ask Simon about that moment. [7] It was a great conversation. Here's an excerpt of what he shared:

Paul: *Simon, tell us about how you handled that weird moment where there was a little bit of a mic issue and they had to hand off a new mic to you.*

Simon: *Yeah, my mic was making funny crackling sounds when I was going and so they had to actually change my mic in the middle of my talk. It's all on the video. You can see it all. They didn't edit it out. And I love that!*

The reason I love that is because, you know whether it's a TED X or another presentation, people are so worried about their PowerPoints being perfect, or the slides going in the right order, and they freak out as if that's what makes a presentation.

And I'm living proof that if everything goes horribly wrong, you can still become one of the most popular TED Talks of all time. You know it's like my microphone breaks, the audio quality is pretty junk throughout the whole thing, and yet still people want to see it. So, it's what you bring to the table and it's the passion you bring to the table, not just how well your slides go that makes the difference.

I think his comments are powerful. Let me echo again what he said, "It's what you bring to the table. It's your passion, not just how well your slides go that make the difference." Passion makes the difference in helping you to pivot.

One more thing on pivoting. Keep in mind again that there are different personality styles and learning styles in the audience. Speakers able to pivot resonate the most with those who are high D's. "D" stands for Dominance. These audience members place emphasis on accomplishing results, getting to the bottom line, and value confidence.

The D's are the ones who want to accept challenges, and often they like to see how others succeed in the midst of it. When you pivot and keep your composure you are satisfying and directly connecting with the D's. For most speakers, that's a tough thing.

Simon's talk serves as great reminder to keep your cool no matter what. The key is to continue to show your passion while you stay connected and focused with your audience. In addition to passion, another mechanism to help you best pivot and plow forward is described in the next chapter.

Chapter 8
Iterate the Point

If you can't write your message in a sentence,
you can't say it in an hour.

— Dianna Booher

D id you notice the phrase that gets the biggest payoff in Simon's TED Talk? It's the one he repeats the most.

"People don't buy what you do, they buy why you do it."

It took Simon over 4 minutes to set the table before he made his key statement. Then, once he did, he was able to reuse it again and again. But it's not just how often he said it, it's how he said.

First though, watch how he follows the pattern of framing, stories and science, and then reminds the audience of the key point. To drive a *message* home, you should do the same. Then learn to iterate the point. And make sure your key thought can be said in one sentence; like Simon's.

I know what you might be thinking, "But Simon's talk is 18 minutes long!" True, and every bit of it is good, but keep in mind his key point is only 4 seconds long, and that includes the pause. Look at it again:

"People don't buy what you do,
they buy why you do it."

There are two parts to Simon's key point. The first part identifies the principal dilemma. I call this the *setup.*

"People don't buy what you do,"

The *setup* grabs our attention. As an audience, we subconsciously lean forward a little on the setup. We wonder, *what might be coming next?*

After a short pause, Simon hints at the answer to our silent question with a *truth drop.*

"They buy why you do it."

The *truth drop* triggers an epiphany for the audience. It creates in us a new perspective.

A key point, like Simon's, should contain an insight that first reveals a dilemma in the *setup* and then a forgotten secret in the *truth drop.* Key points have only one goal; to empower them! If a key point, doesn't empower, it's not a key point.

Consider some of the greatest quotes of all time, which have this pattern of a *setup* followed by a *truth drop.* As speakers, we can learn from these examples.

	Setup (before the pause)	Truth Drop (after the pause)	Communicator
1	*"Ask not what your country can do for you*	*but what you can do for your country?"*	– John F. Kennedy
2	*"Be yourself;"*	*everyone else is already taken."*	– Oscar Wilde
3	*"Change your thoughts*	*and you change your world."*	– Norman Vincent Peale
4	*"Do not let what you cannot do*	*interfere with what you can do."*	– John Wooden
5	*"For every minute you are angry*	*you lose sixty seconds of happiness."*	– Ralph Waldo Emerson

6	"If opportunity doesn't knock,	build a door."	– Milton Berle
7	"If you cannot do great things,	do small things in a great way."	– Napoleon Hill
8	"If you want to lift yourself up,	lift up someone else."	– Booker T. Washington
9	"Life has no limitations,	except the ones you make"	– Les Brown
10	"Live as if you were to die tomorrow.	Learn as if you were to live forever."	– Mahatma Gandhi
11	"No one can make you feel inferior	without your consent."	– Eleanor Roosevelt
12	"People don't buy what you do,	they buy why you do it."	– Simon Sinek
13	"People will forget what you said, people will forget what you did,	but people will never forget how you made them feel."	– Maya Angelou
14	"The best way to predict the future	is to invent it."	– Alan Kay
15	"The difference between ordinary and extraordinary	is that little extra."	– Jimmy Johnson
16	"The only thing we have to fear	is fear itself."	– Franklin D. Roosevelt
17	"Too many of us are not living our dreams	because we are living our fears."	– Les Brown
18	"You only live once,	but if you do it right, once is enough."	– Mae West

Like these great communicators, remind the audience of your key point using a similar convention. Make it meaningful and memorable by using this simple formula: a *set up* followed by a *truth drop*.

Next, iterate your key point – share it again. But be sure it resonates with your audience when you use it. Timing is everything. For Simon, his key point anchored every story. That's because the message you want others "to get" happens best if you repeat it in the context of a story or the scientific research. Again, you must iterate!

A clear message shared repeatedly creates the greatest stimuli for your audience – it makes it more memorable. That's the goal of every speaker; to share something that an audience will not forget. Typically, people have to hear your message seven times before they remember. Some experts say it's more. Simon, however, pulls it off in five before he reframes it in a different way at the end.

There is value in iterating for all personality types. For D's it helps them see the Big Picture. For I's it feeds their enthusiasm. For S's it clearly indicates steadiness. And for C's it shows a conscientious approach by the speaker when he or she repeats the point.

Like Simon, once you make your key point, iterate on this pattern as frequently as you can. Make it universal. Simon shares the same key point against the backdrop of four different stories: Apple Computer, the Wright Brothers, TiVo, and Martin Luther King, Jr. Each story authenticated his message. He also used scientific research and some humor to hammer it home. As a result, he connects with all the different personality styles. Arguably, it's clear that his goal was to reiterate on the key point. Make your speech more effective by doing the same.

As you prepare for your next speech, you may feel compelled to avoid repeating your key point. However, remind yourself of the benefit when you iterate. An audience will appreciate a familiar and fresh story that emphasizes and reminds them of the key point. For a speaker, it's how you make your message remarkable.

Chapter 9
Play the Guitar

Someone told me the smile on my face gets bigger
when I play the guitar.

— Niall Horan

I know what you might be thinking. *"Guitar? Simon doesn't use a guitar. That's crazy."* Well, that's true. He doesn't play a guitar in his TED Talk, but he does use a few instruments to help deliver his message with clarity. He uses a flip chart and a magic pen. He also uses his body language.

I share the phrase "play the guitar," because that's what artists with stage presence do -- at least metaphorically. If you ever watch a show like *The Voice* or *American Idol*, you'll notice that the standout performers aren't the ones just using their mic to sing, they are doing something or using something beyond just their voice to connect with the audience. I call it *playing the guitar*, but it doesn't have to be a guitar. It can be any instrument or resource -- including a make-believe object in the room. Great performers chose to be vulnerable by doing something different to create connection.

Think of it this way; those that play a guitar are often taking a risk. It's one more thing that might not go right, but it's also the one thing that might make a difference. Those willing to stand out are more authentic and simply connect better with the audience. Singers sing, but performers perform. One's like Karaoke, the other is like a Concert that you'll never forget. Ask yourself, would you rather be known as a safe Karaoke Speaker, or an unforgettable Impact Speaker?

As Impact Speakers, we can learn something from Simon's model. Impact Speakers take risks. For example, if you are a visual learner and thinker, a whiteboard or flip chart might be just what you need to help deliver a solid speech. But Karaoke Speakers, they don't like to take that risk. They would rather use PowerPoint.

Can I just say up front? PowerPoint doesn't really count. While it might be an instrument, most people use it as a crutch. It's not really powerful – at least the way most people use it.

PowerPoint is more like a programmed drum machine. It has little soul to it. It's not being used to perform, it's being used to play and placate a Karaoke Speaker. A drum machine detracts, but real drums – real instruments -- now that creates a more emotional experience for an audience.

My recommendation is this. Don't use PowerPoint unless you have to. Simon doesn't -- at least not in this TED Talk -- he uses a flip chart, his magic pen and well-timed gestures with his hands and face.

If you do choose to use PowerPoint, don't let the PowerPoint drive your speech. That's Karaoke. Instead, use your speech to drive your PowerPoint. For example, in your slides, see if you can use it without bullets and a mass of words. Use images instead! I know it's a risk – a wordless slide -- but they are so much more powerful.

If necessary, ask yourself, do I really need PowerPoint? Watch again what Simon does. Remember, he's not using it, therefore why should you?

Instead of PowerPoint, Simon draws a simple set of concentric circles on the flip chart using a magic pen he labels: *Why*, *How*, and

What. He then refers to his drawing during his talk. This diagram of The Golden Circle helps drive his point home – especially when he iterates the key point. Without even having to say the words, he can now point his magic pen at the flip chart to emphasize the core message.

> *"People don't buy <u>what</u> you do, they buy <u>why</u> you do it."*

As you read and hear the phrase, can you imagine Simon's Golden Circle drawing and him pointing to the *what* and *why* circles? He has used this figurative guitar to connect you and move you. You can do the same as a speaker. Be sure to practice ahead of time though. You don't want to look like a singer holding a guitar not knowing how to play. Practice. Practice. Practice. And keep it simple!

When it comes to speaking, there is value in *playing the guitar* figuratively for all personality types.

For D's, the passion of the speaker *playing the guitar* mirrors the drive they also have. They are excited you are being creative.

For I's, *playing the guitar* feeds their enthusiasm. They will be satisfied you are bringing them into the experience.

For S's, *playing the guitar* exhibits an approach that more easily conveys the information, which is what they want. They will be hoping to you see succeed.

For C's, *playing the guitar* reflects a quality and competency that separates you as a speaker from the rest. The will be watching to support your performance and give you their praise.

Keep in mind your audience reflects all these temperaments. None of us are just one type, but any one of us will have one behavior more prevalent than the other. Know your priority type. If you are a "D" or an "I", *playing the guitar* will be easier, because of your willingness to take risk. If you are an "S" or "C", you may be more risk adverse. For the S's and C's in the audience, just remember they want to see you do well. As my wife reminds me, "Give yourself permission to be BOLD."

You may wonder, *what instruments can I use?* Well, other than a flipchart there are lots of other mechanisms you can use too. It can be a simple prop, or even a section of the stage that you let people imagine being something else. I've seen people use ropes. I've seen a mystery box. I've even seen a can of soup used to emphasize a point.

Just be creative. Be interesting. Be different! It's how you connect!

Chapter 10
Thank the Audience

Take time to be kind and to say, 'thank you.'

— Zig Ziglar

Finally, did you notice how Simon closes his speech by thanking the audience? Some presentation gurus believe this is a cardinal sin of speaking, but I disagree. The audience needs a final trigger at the end to know when the full message has been delivered.

Imagine a rock star walking off the stage at the end of a big show without thanking the audience for them coming. You would probably wonder if he and the band were actually done, or they just grew tired and left, right?

When the front man of the band thanks the audience, then you know they truly valued the presence of all those that are there. It makes you feel good. As a speaker, why wouldn't you want to do the same thing?

Author Jeremey Donovan in his ground-breaking book, *How to Deliver a TED Talk*, observes that almost every TED speaker ends their talk with *thank you.* [8] He supports you doing the same. However, Donovan reminds you that, "The conclusion is your final opportunity to inspire your audience." So, before you say *thank you*, make sure you leave them a clear call to action; "an idea worth spreading." Only then is it okay to finish with *thank you*.

The value in giving thanks resonates most for those with a personality type of an S. "S" stands for Steadiness. These audience members value cooperation, sincerity and dependability. Once again, they prefer a calm manner and approach, which is the effect of gratitude. They thrive on supportive actions. But truth be told, all personality styles value appreciation.

Thanking the audience is like putting a bow on a package. It causes the audience to respond with gratitude themselves. It's one simple way to finish with grace.

Be Credible

The hallmark of a great speech is its persuasion.
It's what it's all about.

— Unknown

Persuasion is achieved by the speaker's personal
character when the speech is so spoken as to
make us think him credible. We believe good men
more fully and more readily than others.

— Aristotle

C redible. I love this word. It means someone who is trustworthy, honest, and believable. As we close out this book, recognize that the mark of a great speech is measured by the credibility of the speaker. Credibility is within your grasp. Credibility is a choice.

Speaking of choice, do you see how simple, yet powerful Simon's model can be to help you be persuasive? You can do this too. His model is scalable for any presentation.

As final guidance, let's take a moment to review the key elements of the Speech Blueprint:

1. **Deliver Dips and Spikes** – Show the heartbeat of your message. A heartbeat is going to have dips and spikes. The dips and spikes of your speech reflect your passion, and the message of your heart. If there are no dips or

spikes, then there is no heartbeat. If there's no heartbeat, then there's no impact.

2. **Frame with Questions** – A well placed question creates an invitation for the audience to participate. Thought provoking questions set you up for creating big payoffs.

3. **Follow with Stories** – Stories give context to your message and make it interesting. Remember Les Brown's advice, "Never make a point without a story, and never tell a story without a point." A great story makes it memorable.

4. **Share the Science** – Compelling evidence always demands a favorable verdict. Use scientific research to strengthen your message. It will help you in your credibility.

5. **Inject Real Humor** – A good laugh here and there makes your message taste like good medicine. As Ken Davis shares, "It softens the heart." You don't need jokes; just point out the funny oddities of life - especially the ones you've experienced.

6. **Insert Timely Pauses** – Create cues for reflection through subtle gaps in your message. This will increase your ability to create a heartfelt connection for your audience.

7. **Pivot Through Problems** – Challenges will come but resolve yourself ahead of time to roll with the punches. Recognize that a little bit of roughness makes you more authentic and more liked if you keep your cool.

8. **Iterate the Point** – Often times the audience won't get the key message until they hear it multiple times. For

example, Simon's point, "People don't buy what you do, they buy why you do it," is iterated five times but it never gets old. Be clear on what that point is, and then repeat it as necessary.

9. **Play the Guitar** – This is a figurative term. A great presenter is willing to use other instruments – other tools -- during the talk to deliver the message – not just the mic. The key is to not use too many instruments, just a few. It can be a flip chart, a simple prop, or even a section of the stage that you let people imagine as something else. Don't forget to use well-timed gestures including your hands and facial expressions.

10. **Thank the Audience** – The final word to close as a last line is to show your appreciation for the audience's time. It's a mark of integrity, achieved simply by thanking them for their attention. This moment of grace will be reciprocated by them showing you their gratitude and thanks. It's the connection everyone desires.

Well, that's it. Those are the ten elements from Simon's speech. In addition to Simon's TED Talk, there is a wealth of other great TED Talks that you can evaluate as well, many of which are good models for crafting and delivering a persuasive speech. I think you'll find most of the popular ones have elements of what Simon demonstrates for us. Your next presentation can too!

For more insights on leadership, be sure to visit speechblueprint.com. I would love to hear from you!

Thank you and God bless!

Paul

Appendix A - Speech Rewind

The full speech of Simon's TED Talk was too big for my short chapters, but I still want you to have easy access to it. This is my best effort to transcribe his talk. I used this to plot out the Speech EKG you saw in Chapter 1 and used it for all my analysis that followed. I know there are a few words from his talk that might be missing, but the majority of his message is here.

As you explore the table, compare the times of the dips and spikes from the EKG with this table. The text in red indicate questions he asked (framing), whereas the text in blue indicate his key premise and takeaway that he wanted to leave the audience to remember (key point).

I hope you enjoy the elements of his speech that have been transcribed below!

Time-In (minute mark)	Text / Event (actions, points, takeaways, response)	Resonance (impact value)
0.23	*Simon is welcomed w/ applause...*	6
0.33	**How do you explain when things don't go as we assumed?**	-3
0.47	Or Better, **How do you explain when others are able to achieve things that seem to defy all the assumptions?**	-4
0.55	For example, **Why is Apple so innovative?**	-5

0.67	Yet they are just a computer company; they are just like everyone else. **Why is it they have something different?**	-4
1	**Why is it that Martin Luther King led the civil rights movement?**	-4
1.3	**Why is it that the Wright Brothers were able to figure out controlled powered man flight when there were other teams more qualified?**	-5
1.33	[HOOK} **There's something else at play here!**	7
1.42	About 3 1/2 Years ago I made a discovery	7
1.63	This discovery profoundly changed my view on how I thought the world worked. And it even profoundly changed the way in which I operate in it.	6
1.85	As it turns out there's a pattern -- ALL THE GREAT and INSPIRING LEADERS and ORGANIZATIONS -- they all think, act and communicate the exact same way.	5
1.92	And it's the complete opposite to everyone else.	6
2	All I did was CODIFY it - and it's probably the world's simplest idea.	3
2.22	*Simon goes to white board.* "I call it **The Golden Circle**" *He draws three circles and labels them.* *WHY - HOW - WHAT*	6
2.33	This little idea explains why some organizations and some leaders are able to inspire whereas others aren't.	6

2.47	Every person / organization on the planet knows WHAT they do. 100% *(Simon is pointing at the WHAT circle)*	6
2.52	Some know HOW they do it *(Simon is pointing at the HOW circle)*	5
2.67	Very few people or organizations know WHY they do what they do.	6
2.83	By "Why", I mean **What's your purpose?** **What's your cause?** **What's your belief?**	-7
2.87	**Why does your organization exist?**	-6
2.92	**Why do you get out bed in the morning?**	-6
2.95	**And why should anyone care?**	-6
3.08	The way we think, the way we act, the way we communicate is all from the outside in, it's obvious. We go from the clearest thing to the fuzziest thing.	6
3.27	**But the inspired leaders / the inspired organizations regardless of their size / regardless of their industry all think, act and communicate from the inside out.**	9
3.63	[STORY] Let me give you an example. I use Apple because they're easy to understand and everybody gets it. If Apple were like everyone else, a marketing message might sound like this...	6

	[WHAT] *We make great computers.* [HOW] *They are beautifully designed, simple to use, and user friendly.* *Want to buy one?* EEEGGH. *(Simon shrugs shoulder)*	
3.83	That's how most of us communicate! We say what we do. We say how we are different or how we are better, then we expect some sort of behavior [to result].	6
4.07	IT'S UNINSPIRING	4
4.43	Here's how Apple actually communicates. [WHY] *Everything we do we believe in challenging the status quo. We believe in thinking differently.*	9
	[HOW] *The way we challenge the status quo is making our products beautifully designed, simple to use, and user friendly.*	
	[WHAT] *We just happen to make great computers.* *Want to buy one?*	
4.48	**Totally Different, Right?**	-6
4.53	All I did was reverse the order of the information.	7
4.65	What it proves to us is that people don't buy what you do - they buy why you do it. *[CIRCLES WHITE BOARD]*	10
	People Don't Buy What You Do - They Buy Why You Do It!	

4.9	This explains why we are comfortable buying a computer from Apple. An MP3 from Apple. Or a Phone from Apple.	5
5.07	But there's nothing that distinguishes them structurally from their competitors. Their competitors are all equally qualified to make all of these products. In fact, they tried.	4
5.23	[STORY] GATEWAY example - Flat screen TVs - nobody bought one	4
5.48	DELL example - MP3 and PDAs - nobody bought one.	4
5.67	People don't buy what you do, they buy why you do it!	10
5.83	The goal is not to do business with everybody who needs what you have. The goal is to do business with people who believe what you believe.	6
5.87	Here's is the Best Part...	7
6	[SCIENCE/ RESEARCH OBSERVATION] None of what I am telling you is my opinion, it's all grounded in the tenets of biology. Not psychology -- BIOLOGY.	5
6.17	If you look at the cross section of the human brain, you'll see that it's broken up into three major components that parlay perfectly with the Golden Circle.	5
6.27	The Neocortex corresponds with the WHAT level.	5

6.37	It's responsible for our rational and analytical thought and language.	5
6.45	The middle two sections [HOW & WHY] make up our Limbic brains.	4
6.53	The Limbic brain is responsible for all of our feelings. Like Trust and loyalty.	4
6.57	It's also responsible for All Human Behavior.	5
6.6	...All Decision Making.	5
6.65	...And it has no capacity for language.	5
6.83	In other words. When we communicate from the outside in (*Simon is pointing to flip chart*). Yes, people can understand vast amounts of complicated information like features and benefits and facts and figures. It just doesn't drive behavior.	4
7	[But] when we communicate from the inside out, we're talking DIRECTLY to part of the brain that controls behavior and we allow people to rationalize it with the tangible things that we say and do.	6
7.03	This is where gut decisions come from	5
7.18	I know what all the facts and details say, but It just doesn't feel right. **Why would we use that verb?** It doesn't feel right.	-4
7.33	Because the part of the brain that controls decision making, doesn't control language. And the best we can muster up is "I don't know. It just doesn't feel right." [Good facial usage]	4

7.5	Sometimes we say we are leading with our heart or we are leading with our soul. ... it's all happening in your limbic brain.	4
7.55	The part of the brain that controls decision making and not language	5
7.82	But if you don't know WHY you do what you do,	-4
	and people respond to WHY you do what you do,	
	then **HOW will you ever get anybody to vote for you?**	
	- buy from you?	
	- or more importantly be loyal and want to be a part of what it is that you do?	
7.92	The goal is NOT to sell people who need WHAT you have *[The WHAT]*.	8
	The goal is to sell to people who BELIEVE in what you believe *[The WHY]*	
8.02	The goal is not just to hire people who need a job. It's to hire people who believe what you believe.	4
8.25	If you hire people who just because they can do a job they'll work for your money, but if you hire people who believe in what you believe they'll work for you with blood sweat and tears.	4
8.28	[STORY]	6
	Nowhere is there a better example of this than there is with the Wright Brothers.	

8.35	Most people don't know about Samuel Pierpont Langley. *(Set Up for story...)*	3
8.48	Back in the early part of the 20th century, the pursuit of powered man flight was like the DOT COM of the day. Everybody was trying it!	4
8.57	Samuel Pierpont Langley had what we assumed to be the recipe for success.	3
8.77	When you ask someone *now why did your product or why did your company fail?* They'll always give you the same permutation of the same three things: • Undercapitalized, • the Wrong People, • Bad Market Conditions.	-4
8.95	Samuel Pierpont Langley was given $50,000 by the War Department to figure out this flying machine. Money was no problem.	3
9.07	He held a seat at Harvard, and worked at the Smithsonian, and was EXTREMELY well connected. He knew all the big minds of the day.	3
9.18	He hired the best minds that money could find. And the market conditions were FANTASTIC.	4
9.27	The New York Times followed him around everywhere, and everyone was routing for Langley.	4

9.32	But how come we have never heard of Samuel Pierpont Langley?	-5
9.55	A few hundred miles away in Dayton Ohio. Orville and Wilbur Wright. They had none of we consider to be the recipe for success. They had no money. They paid for their dream with the proceeds from the bicycle shop	5
9.6	Not a single person on the Wright brothers team had a college education.	5
9.63	Not even Orville or Wilbur.	5
9.68	And the New York Times followed them around nowhere.	6
9.8	The difference was that Orville and Wilbur were driven by a cause, a purpose, a belief.	6
9.9	They believed that if they could figure out this flying machine, it would change the course of the world.	5
10.1	Samuel Pierpont Langley was different. He wanted to be rich and he wanted to be famous. He was in pursuit of the results [the WHAT]. He was in pursuit of the riches. And low and behold -- look what happened!	3
10.25	The people who believed in the Wright Brothers dream, worked with them with blood, sweat and tears. The others -- Langley's guys -- worked just for the paycheck.	5

10.38	And they tell stories of how every time the Wright brothers went out, they would have to take five sets of parts, because that's how many times they would crash before they came in for supper.	5
10.57	Eventually, on December 17th, 1903, the Wright brothers took flight, and no one was there to even experience it. We found out about it a few days later.	4
10.73	Further proof that Langley was motivated by the wrong thing, the day the Wright brothers took flight, he quit!	3
10.88	He could have said, "That's an amazing discovery guys, and I will improve upon your technology," but he didn't. He wasn't first, he didn't get rich, he didn't get famous, so he quit.	3
10.95	People don't buy what you do; they buy why you do it.	10
11.03	And **if you talk about what you believe,** **you will attract those who believe what you believe.**	6
11.1	But why is it important to attract those who believe what you believe?	-4
11.17	[SCIENCE/ RESEARCH OBSERVATION] Something called the law of diffusion of innovation. *(new flip board chart is started)*	2

11.2	If you don't know the law, you definitely know the terminology.	3
11.28	The first two and a half percent of our population are our **innovators**.	3
11.37	The next 13 and a half percent of our population are our **early adopters.**	4
11.45	The next 34 percent are your early majority, your **late majority and your laggards.**	4
11.53	The only reason these people buy touch tone phones is because you can't buy rotary phones anymore. (LAUGHTER)	6
11.88	What the law of diffusion of innovation tells us is that if you want mass-market success or mass-market acceptance of an idea, you cannot have it until you achieve this tipping point between 15 and 18 percent market penetration.	4
11.93	Then the system tips.	4
12	I love asking businesses, *"What's your conversion on new business?"* Oh, and they tell me *"it's about 10%..."*	-3
12.23	Well, you can trip over 10 percent of the customers. We all have about 10 percent who just "get it." **That's how we describe them, right?**	-3

	That's like that gut feeling, "Oh, they just get it."	
12.33	So, **it's this here, this little gap,** that you have to close.	3
	As Geoffrey Moore calls it, "Crossing the chasm."	
12.47	Because, you see, **the early majority will not** **try something until someone else has tried** **it first.**	6
12.57	And these guys, the innovators and the early adopters, they're comfortable making those gut decisions.	3
12.72	They're more comfortable making those intuitive decisions that are driven by what they believe about the world and not just what product is available.	4
12.83	These are the people who stood in line for six hours to buy an iPhone when they first came out, when you could have just walked into the store the next week and bought one off the shelf.	5
12.97	These are the people who spent 40,000 dollars on flat screen TVs when they first came out, even though the technology was substandard.	5
13.07	Oh, by the way, they didn't do it because the technology was so great. **They did it for themselves!**	7
13.12	**It's because they wanted to be first.**	7

13.13	People don't buy what you do; they buy why you do it.	10
13.23	And what you do simply PROVES what you believe.	8
13.27	In fact, people will do the things that prove what they believe.	6
13.48	The reason that person bought the iPhone in the first six hours, stood in line for six hours, was because of what they believed about the world, and how they wanted everybody to see them. **They were First!**	7
13.52	People don't buy what you do; they buy why you do it.	10
13.63	So, let me give you a famous example, a famous failure and a famous success of the law of diffusion of innovation.	3
13.8	First, the famous failure.	4
	[STORY]	
	It's a commercial example. As we said before, a second ago, the recipe for success is money and the right people and the right market conditions. Right? You should have success then!	
13.85	Look at TIVO	4
14	From the time TiVo came out, about eight or nine years ago, to this current day, they are the single highest-quality product on the market, hands down, there is no dispute.	5
14.1	They were extremely well-funded. Market conditions were fantastic. I mean, we use TiVo as verb.	6

14.15	I TiVo stuff on my piece of junk Time Warner DVR all the time. **(LAUGHTER)**	6
14.23	But TiVo's a commercial failure	5
14.27	They've never made money.	4
14.38	And when they went IPO, their stock was at about 30 or 40 dollars and then plummeted, and it's never traded above 10.	3
14.45	In fact, I don't even think it's traded above six, except for a couple of little spikes.	3
14.53	You see, when TiVo launched their product, they told us all what they had.	4
14.7	They said, "We have a product that pauses live TV, skips commercials, rewinds live TV and memorizes your viewing habits without you even asking."	4
14.83	And the cynical majority said, "We don't believe you. We don't need it. We don't like it..."	3
14.87	You're scaring us."	4
15.07	What if they had said, "If you're the kind of person who likes to have total control over every aspect of your life, boy, do we have a product for you.	5
15.15	It pauses live TV, skips commercials, memorizes your viewing habits, etc., etc."	5
15.18	**People don't buy what you do; they buy why you do it.**	10

15.25	And what you do simply serves as the proof of what you believe.	7
15.33	[STORY] Now let me give you a successful example of the law of diffusion of innovation.	5
15.5	In the summer of 1963, 250,000 people showed up on the mall in Washington to hear Dr. King speak.	6
15.62	They sent out no invitations, and there was no website to check the date.	6
15.65	**How do you do that?**	-6
15.73	Well, Dr. King wasn't the only man in America who was a great orator.	5
15.78	He wasn't the only man in America who suffered in a pre-civil rights America.	5
15.83	In fact, some of his ideas were bad.	5
15.87	But he had a gift.	6
15.97	He didn't go around telling people what needed to change in America. He went around and told people what he believed."	6
16.02	"I believe, I believe, I believe," he told people.	7
16.12	And people who believed what he believed took his cause, and they made it their own, and they told people.	7
16.2	And some of those people created structures to get the word out to even more people.	5

16.35	And low and behold, 250,000 people showed up on the right day, at the right time, to hear him speak.	7
16.42	**How many of them showed up for him?**	-7
16.43	ZERO	8
16.47	**They showed up for themselves.**	10
16.6	It's what they believed about America that got them to travel in a bus for eight hours, to stand in the sun in Washington in the middle of August.	8
16.7	It's what they believed, and it wasn't about black versus white. 25 percent of the audience was white.	7
16.83	Dr. King believed that there are two types of laws in this world, those that are made by a higher authority and those that are made by man.	5
16.97	And not until all the laws that are made by man are consistent with the laws that are made by the higher authority, will we live in a just world.	6
17.07	It just so happened that the Civil Rights Movement was the perfect thing to help him bring his cause to life.	6
17.12	We followed, not for him, but for ourselves.	7

17.22	And, by the way, he gave the "I have a dream" speech, not the "I have a plan" speech. (LAUGHTER)	8
17.33	Listen to politicians now with their comprehensive 12-point plans. They're not inspiring anybody.	6
17.38	There are leaders and there are those who lead.	7
17.45	Leaders hold a position of power or authority.	7
17.52	**But those who lead inspire us.**	7
17.65	Whether they're individuals or organizations, **we follow those who lead, not because we have to, but because we want to.**	8
17.75	**We follow those who lead, not for them, but for ourselves.**	9
17.93	And it's those who start with "why" that have the ability to inspire those around them or find others who inspire them.	9
17.97	Thank you very much.	9
18.02	(APPLAUSE)	10

Appendix B - EKG Your Speech

*S**how us how to create a Speech EKG of our own?** That was the suggestion my editing team recommended after reviewing an early version of this manuscript.

I definitely want to show you how, but first I want to give credit where credit is due. The Speech EKG concept is not entirely my creation. One of my mentors Roddy Galbraith, who is arguably the best coach in the art of speaking, uses a very similar model to train others. Roddy studies speeches of influential speakers. He has mastered the art of decomposing a great speech into elements and teaching it in a compelling way. [9]

One of the methods Roddy uses is to show visually the payoffs of a message. The visualization shows the importance of organizing a presentation with stories and spacing *takeaways* to create a strong heartbeat that iterates throughout a message. For me, that's where the idea of a Speech EKG was inspired -- or at least evolved.

I have seen Roddy create an EKG of some of the best communicators in the world including John C. Maxwell and Les Brown. In this book, I present a slightly different EKG method, but it is very similar in intent. *Roddy, if you are reading this, thank you for your insight and inspiring others in the art of speaking*!

So, now let's walk through the steps in how you can do it.

STEP 1 - Setup Your Table

Appendix A provides a table that you can follow as a model to map your speech. I built it in Excel, which makes it easy to replicate.

This table provides three essential components for creating an EKG: *time-in*, *text/event*, and *resonance*.

- **Time-In** is the time of the speech where Simon (or the audience) took an action, made a statement, or asked a question.

- **Text / Event** is simply that. It is either the text of the speech broken down representing a statement or question, or a note of the audience's response.

- **Resonance** is a subjective measure of the amount of impact that the text or event has on the audience. The *resonance*, once you map it, either falls below or above the midline depending if it was a *question*, a *statement*, or even a well-timed *pause*. We'll address this again in a moment.

Additionally, what you don't see in the table are two hidden columns used to properly capture the time.; a *minute* column and a *seconds* column used to mark the real time components of the speech. These are used to calculate the values for the *time-in* column, which is then used to plot out the EKG graph. To calculate this value, a simple equation is used that couples the *minutes* value with the *seconds* value. For those curious, here's the formula:

$$\text{Time-In} = ((\text{MinuteValue} * 60) + \text{SecondValue}) / 60$$

To make it easy, I've posted a Speech EKG Excel Template file as a download for your speeches that you can use too. Just go to the *Speech Blueprint* website at *www.speechblueprint.com*. It has embedded in it this formula and a way to plot your speech.

STEP 2 - Transcribe Your Speech

I recommend a service like Rev at *www.rev.com* to extract the words from your recorded speech. They magically take your MP3 file and within a few hours create a transcript of your talk. The cost is about a dollar a minute.

The other way to do it is you can do what I did and transcribe the speech on your own. While it takes a long time, you might gain deeper insight in the listen -- like the power of pauses.

I actually transcribed Simon's speech way back in 2013 on a long a flight from Washington DC to San Diego; the flight had no wi-fi or in-flight entertainment, so I had nothing to distract me other than a crying baby two seats back. Years later, I discovered someone had already transcribed and published Simon's speech. Now you can easily find the transcript on the TED web site along with Simon's video.

Whatever way you extract the words and elements of the speech, each sentence is a candidate for each of the rows in your table.

STEP 3 - Map Your Speech

Using Excel, I unhid the *minute* and *second* columns, and marked the time of the speech against the words as I listened to it. Simultaneously, I entered the *resonance* values of Simon's TED Talk marked against the time/event in the speech.

Ultimately, this is what was used to generate the graph you saw in Chapter 1 -- aka the Speech EKG. You can do the same for your speech too. It's just a simple 2-D line chart with the *time-in* values on the X axis, and the *resonance* values plotted on the Y axis. The negative and positive resonance are what creates the heartbeat.

To understand these heartbeats, let me back up for minute. I should mention that as I listened and analyzed Simon's speech, I did two things concurrently:

(1) I marked the time in the first two columns when he spoke the transcribed words (*minutes* and *seconds*). Because I had the formula plugged in, the magic of Excel atomically calculated the *time-in* value, which I needed later for graphing.

(2) At that *time-in* mark in his speech, I performed a subjective evaluation of his speech. Specifically, in the *resonance* column, I identified the value of his remarks as it impacted the audience. *Resonance* was either negative (for dips) or positive (for spikes).

Negative Resonance is not a Bad Thing

Did you happen to notice that when Simon posed a question, it fell below the midline with a negative value between -1 and -7?

This is based on its strength and weight. Negative doesn't necessarily mean bad. The more impactful the question the more "below the line" resonance it will have. Now, if Simon had demanded a "reactive response" of the audience using a question followed by a long pause, the resonance may have likely scored a -8 to a -10. But that's not always Simon's style. He uses thinking questions to frame his stories and key points, whether the audience answers verbally or not.

Well timed pauses, by the way, can also be scored as negative resonance, which again is not bad. During the course of your speech, values should be marked negative if the inquiry or pause challenges or alters a person's belief or present state.

Positive Resonance leads to Payoffs

If it was not a question, then the *resonance* value likely landed above the midline with a positive value between 1 and 10. The more impactful the point the more positive resonance it contains. Roddy calls these big spikes "payoffs."

The way to think about is this way: it's positive *resonance* if the element of speech affirms or raises a person's belief or awareness. Well timed pauses that connect the audience in this way can generate positive *resonance* also. The pause in this case isn't changing their state -- it doesn't make them squirm in their seat - instead it's validating their belief.

STEP 4 - Evaluate Your Speech Roddy Style

Once you map your speech and evaluate the graph, you can begin to evaluate it. Ask yourself, does it have a heartbeat? How frequent are the payoffs? Is it balanced?

If you are like me, most likely you'll find some areas that you can improve upon. That's okay. Don't beat yourself up. No speech is perfect, and even if it were, then would it be authentic? Better to deliver an authentic speech than a robotic one. You want to connect with your audience, a little bit of humanness will help with the heartbeat.

To help you better craft a speech with plenty of dips and spikes, I recommend Roddy Galbraith's simple 5 step process. Make sure your speech achieves these objectives:

1. Make a Point
2. Make it Interesting
3. Make it Enjoyable
4. Make it Short
5. Make it Count.

If you evaluate your speech against these components, I believe you'll find you have crafted a speech that truly inspires others.

Wrap Up

Use a Speech EKG to create and map the dips and spikes in your speech giving it a powerful heartbeat. An EKG shows you just how you create life for your audience. And if you really want to take it the next level, I recommend you find a coach - or a mentor like Roddy -- who can help EKG your speech to new heights. Remember, the world is ready to be inspired. Why not let others help you?

Notes

[1] Simon's TED Talk, *How Great Leaders Inspire Action*, available for viewing at https://www.ted.com, recorded in Puget Sound, Washington, Sept 2009.

[2] Matthew E. May, *Winning the Brain Game: Fixing the 7 Fatal Flaws of Thinking*, McGraw-Hill, April 20, 2016.

[3] Warren Berger, *A More Beautiful Question: The Power of Inquiry to Spark Breakthrough Ideas*, Bloomsbury, March 2014.

[4] Diane DiResta, *Les Brown Tells Professional Speakers to Surrender to the Story*, http://bit.ly/2AUSboA, posted Feb 17, 2013, last accessed Jan 22, 2019.

[5] Chip and Dan Heath, *The Power of Moments: Why Great Experiences Have Extraordinary Impact*, Simon & Schuster, Oct 3, 2017.

[6] Ken Davis, *Secrets of Dynamic Communications: Prepare with Focus, Deliver with Clarity, Speak with Power*, Thomas Nelson, 2013.

[7] Paul Gustavson, Barry Smith, and Simon Sinek, *The Platform Builders Discussion with Simon Sinek*, http://bit.ly/PBSimonSinek, recorded March 26, 2014, last accessed Jan 22, 2019.

[8] Jeremey Donovan, *How to Deliver A TED Talk: Secrets of The World's Most Inspiring Presentations*, McGraw-Hill Education, Nov 1, 2013.

[9] John C. Maxwell with Roddy Galbraith, http://bit.ly/2CCdQBX, The John Maxwell Team, last accessed Jan 22, 2019.

SPEECH BLUEPRINT

About the Author

Paul Gustavson is the author of *Leaders Press On*, a founding partner of *The John Maxwell Team*, and a cofounder of SimVentions. SimVentions, is located in Fredericksburg, Virginia, and has been recognized as one of "Virginia's Best Places to Work," and was named by Inc. Magazine as one of "The 50 Best Places to Work in 2016." As the Chief Technology Officer (CTO), Paul leads in identifying and contributing to the company's capability and influencing the strategic vision.

He is a connector and pioneer focused on innovative and relevant ideas that can make an impact. He has also written for numerous journals and several technical books, presents and speaks at conferences domestically and internationally. Paul and his wife live in Virginia.

Additional Resources

- To access additional *Speech Blueprint* resources, and connect with the author, visit www.leaderspresson.com or www.speechblueprint.com.

- To learn more about *SimVentions*, visit www.simventions.com.

- To learn more about *The John Maxwell Team* and discover how to be a better speaker, visit www.johnmaxwellteam.com.

- To learn more about Simon Sinek, visit startwithwhy.com.

- To learn how to organize and shape your speech or book topic using the SCORRE method, which the author recommends, visit www.kendavis.com or www.scorreconference.tv.

Made in the USA
Middletown, DE
02 May 2019